BABY
JESUS

© 1990, 1993 by
THE MOODY BIBLE INSTITUTE
OF CHICAGO

This story has been extracted from
Read Aloud Bible Stories, Vol. 3
by Ella Lindvall

Printed in Mexico

MOODY PRESS

One day God's angel
came to Mary's house.

The angel
had good news
for Mary.
He said,

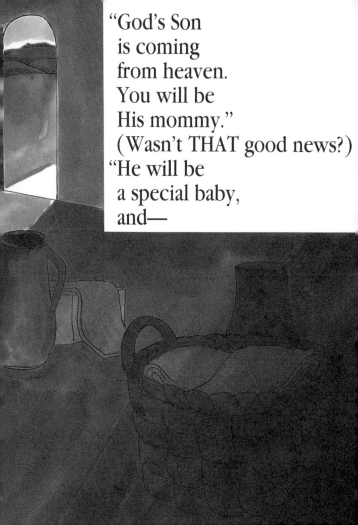

"God's Son
is coming
from heaven.
You will be
His mommy."
(Wasn't THAT good news?)
"He will be
a special baby,
and—

you must name Him
JESUS."
Mary said,
"All right."
Then—

God's angel came
to Joseph's house.
He had
good news
for Joseph.

"Mary will be a mommy," the angel said. "Her baby will be God's Son. He is coming to take away people's badness." (Wasn't THAT good news?)

"You must name
the baby JESUS."
Joseph said,
"All right."
Then one night—

God's angel came to some men on a little hill. The men were taking care of their sheep. The angel said, "I have good news for EVERYBODY.

GOD'S SON
HAS COME
FROM HEAVEN.
He is a baby.
He is sleeping
in a manger."
(That's a box
where donkeys eat.)
All at once—

many angels were there.
In one big voice
they said good things
about God.
After that they went
back home to heaven.
Everything
was quiet again—
as quiet as could be.

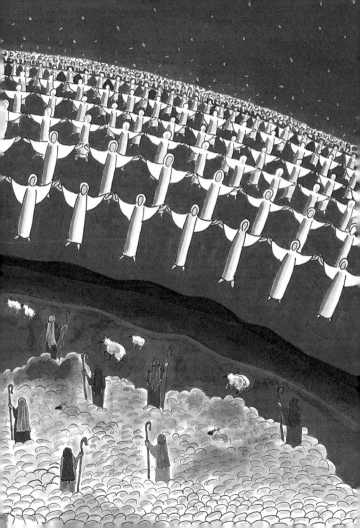

The men looked
at each other.
They said,
"What GOOD NEWS!
Let's find the baby.
Let's go right away.
Let's go fast."
Do you think
they found Him?

They found Him.
There was Mary.
There was Joseph.
And there HE was—
Baby Jesus,
God's Son from heaven—
sleeping in the
manger box.

The men looked
at the baby.
They talked to Mary.
They talked to Joseph.
Then they went back
to their sheep.
Now THEY had
good news to tell.
What was it?

What did you learn?

Jesus came from God.
Jesus came
to grow up
and take away
people's badness.
Yours, too.
And that's good news.

About the Author

Ella K. Lindvall (A.B., Taylor University; Wheaton College; Northern Illinois University) is a mother and former elementary school teacher. She is the author of *The Bible Illustrated for Little Children,* and *Read-Aloud Bible Stories, volumes I, II, and III*.